Flow of thoughts

Kylie Starkey-Brown

Presentation by *BookLeaf Publishing*

Web: www.bookleafpub.com

E-mail: info@bookleafpub.com

ISBN: 9789357690355

First edition 2022

ACKNOWLEDGEMENT

my family
you are my constant

PREFACE

Just a woman who finds recording fragments of thoughts to describe her way in the world, helps her deal with her way in the world.

Children are not ours

Children are not ours

Despite using 'my' or 'ours'
When discussing them.
We do not possess them.
We give them life, and
We are owed nothing.
We should expect nothing.

If we value respect,
We must show them respect.
If we value understanding,
We must first show them understanding.
If we value honesty,
We must be honest with them.
There is no expectation.
No entitlement.

A parent requires no conditions.
Love must flow, constantly.
Love that surrounds,
Following, protecting, energising –
Always available.
Without question.

Our children are not ours.
They are their own.
A sponge,
Soaking up –
Interactions, experiences, connections.
Encourage them.
Support where required.
Lend an ear – always.
Be real.

Be true in your own experiences.
Allow them to collect your experience,
To inform their own.
Step back.
True connection is not expected
Or deserved
It is grown
Through –
Humility
Acceptance.

Be a library.
An easily accessible, reference of experiences.
Ones without sugar-coating.
No shame lies within.
We are all fallible.
A façade of perfection cannot be maintained.
And
It will see them seek the same.

If you have it, let it go –
Allow it to evaporate,
By accepting fault and showing growth. And
Showing love to yourself – as you do others,
So they will too.

And when the time comes,
Load them with love
By answering questions
Examining their fears with them, and
Remaining a constant, flowing and accessible
Source of love

When the time comes,
Even though you'll want to hold them tight,
With both hands.
The urge to protect them from the world
Will rise in your belly
And make you feel like keeping them with you
is best.
It is not,
No matter the tightness and churning,
The longing and yearning.
Swallow it.
Swallow hard.
Breathe deep, exhale hard.
Protection is not your job anymore.
They know.
Seeking their passion, what sets them on fire –

It's not ours to choose.
It is their time.

grateful for gratitude

Grateful for gratitude

How I did suffer
Before I was guided towards gratitude.
The yearning for time travel,
To avoid the pain.
Focusing,
Always,
On the why?
The What if?
Wanting a re-do.
Resenting.
Anguishing.
Whipping myself into a frenzy.
Refusing to accept.

It is not a way to live –

While all days are not rosy,
I am now equipped to cope.
Instead of wishing to go back,
I acknowledge,
Pull apart –
Take the learning I need –
And then look forward.

That is the way I am going after all.
I scan my surroundings.
It is easy to see,
It is everywhere.
So easy to marvel at so many things.
A sunny day without a cloud,
A small moment of connection with someone,
A chance to reflect,
A glass of water,
A message from a loved one.
I could go on –
For a long time,
About all the things to be grateful for,
As there are many -
You just need to look.

Thoughts

Thoughts

Is there a time when our brain is not thinking?
Are dreams thoughts too?
Or are they playing out our thoughts?
Sorting through them,
Bringing things to the forefront.

Sometimes -
The brain is our enemy.
Dredging up the times where -
We felt awkward,
Insufficient,
Ill-prepared,
Unrelatable,
Or dumb,
Just plain dumb.

And then,
Like sticking a fingernail in a papercut –
It finds the one that hurts.
Then,
It replays it –
On repeat.
To ensure you never forget.
The body joins in,
By adding nausea.

And a feeling,
Like you just need to leave –
Get out.
Or quit,
Or break up –
Depending on the situation.

Here it comes again.
Remember when? –
Like you're going to forget?
How.
Can.
You.
Forget?

There it goes again.
Wince.
Regret.
Worry.

And then –
The hindsight comes,
Adding insult to injury.
The fingernail presses harder.
Your conscience alert –
Impressing on your memory,
All the while you are aware –
You're breaking your own heart.

Just a little

Just a little

Wouldn't it be good,
If everyone just showed,
A little kindness.

Take the load off the ones
Who make it their job.
To be kind,
Always.
The ones who have internalised the importance
of kindness.
The ones they say wear rose-coloured glasses.
The ones who are told:
'That's just how it is'
The ones who see through the anger
Of people who hurt them.
Sometimes repeatedly.
They see the pain –
Of the people who believe
'That's just how it is'

They know it can be better.
They know kindness can fill your cup,
Make it overflow.

Surround you with gratitude.
And they know that it isn't hard.
A smile,
A 'good morning'
A cup of coffee,
A genuine 'how are you?'
A compliment.

Just one starts a spark.
More –
Provides the fuel.
Keep going and
You'll fan the flames –
Kindness will set you on fire.
you'll feel alive,
you'll want more.
You'll give more –
Looking for every opportunity to give someone
a simple kindness –
Until it's just what you do.
It would be what everyone does.
Except you think:
"That's just how it is"

Done

Annoyed
Irritated
Clenching jaw, tight shoulders.
Focusing impossible now.
Seek calm.

stress

Stress

Stress is…
Overwhelming thoughts,
Too hard to be prioritised.
Looking, but not seeing.
Needing too much at once.

Stress is…
It is paddling with a fork,
Against the current.
Reaching forward and pulling back –
But going nowhere.
Spinning your wheels.
Constant movement,
But gaining no ground.

Stress is…
Feeling inadequate.
Comparison.
Toxic inner monologue.
Tension building -
Everywhere.
Ready to erupt

Stress is…
Blowing your top.
Spewing forth your internal pressure.
All over someone else.

Stress is…
Acknowledging the guilt after the eruption.
Internalising it.
Adding it to the overwhelm.
Increasing the negative perception of your –
Competence,
Confidence,
And ability.

Stress is…
Contagious

seek the unique

commonness

predictable, obedient

abiding, competing, following

cease camouflaging – start revealing

questioning, accepting, leading

unexpected, curious

uniqueness

Acceptance

Acceptance

You were born,
You exist.
The opinions of others do not refute this.

Take up your space.

Make room for
Your beauty,
Your complexities,
Your passions,
Your struggles,
Your achievements

Do not adjust these to please others.
To do this makes you pliable,
So that you fit in their space.

If you let them -
They'll mould you.

You'll lose your shape.
Your originality suffocates –
Not forging your path.

Rather seeking their acceptance.
Where rules change constantly.
Keeping you on your toes.
Forcing you through their hoops.

The more you comply,
The more they expect.
Small affirmations of your existence may be
given –
But they will not sustain you,
As their acceptance is conditional.
And in you they have found their power.
Exploiting you.

The effort you expend,
To maintain their approval,
Is futile.

They are power-hungry.
An insatiable appetite.
Long ago they sought acceptance,
As you do now.
They expended excessive energy,
failed to maintain acceptance.
It hardened them.
Dried up their exceptionality.
Despondent – they took over what they sought
acceptance from.
Became it –

Loud and brazen,
commanding the attention of all.
Outward they project a show.
Rehearsed to perfection –
Working hard to draw everyone in.
Inward they are hollow.
Stripped of all the niceties – their specialness.
A dark empty space.
Cold and hard –
Belying of their outside.
Loss of attention is perilous.

Acceptance
True acceptance
Comes from within
Nourishes your individuality
Deflects denial from others
Makes you take up your space
And share what you have with others.
Knowing you matter.
Knowing you belong.

confusion to organization

confusion

anxious, erratic

searching, digging, squandering

the plans we make.

locating, placing, accessing

assured, sure

organization

surprise

Surprise friendship
Surprise ending
Or was I the only one surprised?

is it not?

Is it not
Love of yourself
To persist through another day of indecision,
perceived incompetence and inadequacy.
Is it not
love for yourself
That pushes you on, accepting and charging
through your perceived failures and exclusion
Subconsciously realizing, or expecting
That one day –
There'll be more?

Delight

What a delight
Those unexpected moments of sheer excitement
Washing over your body
Touching every cell
Conjuring a squeal of delight
As they leave

Education is experience

Education is experience.
Experience can be gained anywhere –
If one is looking.

competition

Right from birth
We are competing.
Air, Water, Shelter and Food.
A world that claims it is civilised
Is ignoring this

safety

Never have I felt safer
Than when I am wrapped in your arms,
Pulled close to your chest,
Your heart beating a calming rhythm –
Assuring me,
Protecting me,
Saving me.

risk

Does the word serve to remind you
Of the importance of what you stand to lose?
When you seek
something more,
Something different,
To find yourself.
Isn't the real risk
Not finding out?

curse of conversations past

So many tortured souls suffer
after deconstructing social interactions
in hindsight
through the lens of negativity

The Creative Indecisive

27

how wonderful it is to
be flooded with creative ideas
how awful it is to
be paralysed by indecisiveness at the options

Procrastination

To the observer
Is a choice to waste time,
Choosing to avoid what needs to be done
For the procrastinator
It is a mind flooded with ideas
Rushing fast, like a swollen river
They are gone as soon as they come
Impossible to catch.
Brain moving at an incredible pace
Invisible to all around
Take a break
Do an easier task,
One that does not induce a torrent of thoughts

Dear Empath

Be careful.
At times you will tolerate someone
Treating you horribly
Because you understand where it comes from
You,
Their safe place,
Will suffer
And you will reconcile that with their pain.
Remember
Their anger is understandable -
Their cruelty is not.

completion

How wonderful it feels
To not only set yourself a challenge
But to complete it
Completion is a rare thing
For your mind that jumps around
Like a squash ball in a court
Ricocheting from idea to idea
In your head
You rarely stick with a project
To bring all your ideas together
Take a moment
Breathe deep
Look over your work
Acknowledge –
You finished this one!